Terry TRAM! ™
AND MATES

RENA GLENNON

Acknowledging Citation of Learning Resource for Miss Opunti:

Resource: (n.d.). Twinkl; Twinkl Educational Publishing. Retrieved Jan 1, 2024, from https://www.twinkl.co.uk

Copyright © 2024 by Rena Glennon

Hardcover: 978-1-963883-52-7
Paperback: 978-1-963050-88-2
eBook: 978-1-963050-89-9
Library of Congress Control Number: 2024900420

Ordering Information:

Prime Seven Media
518 Landmann St.
Tomah City, WI 54660

Printed in the United States of America

CARBONTHONGS

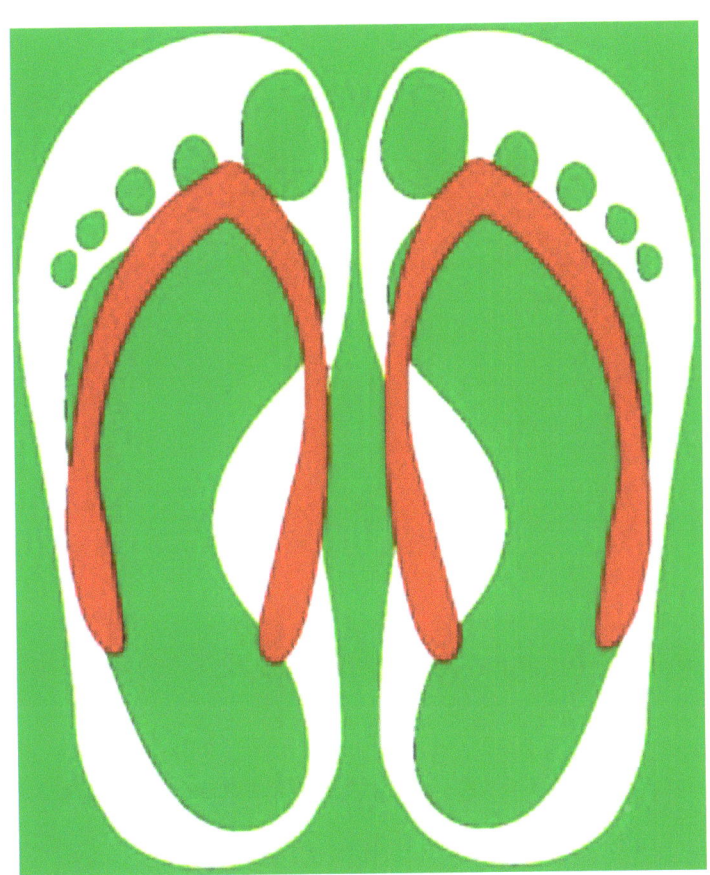

100% GREEN

Terry is proud to be a part of the Green Powered Trams in our Melbourne Network. He now runs entirely, on clean, renewable electricity from solar energy. Melbourne's tram network is now 100 per cent offset by renewable energy thanks to two Victorian solar farms. Foresight Solar Fund powers the entire Melbourne fleet, composed by 450 trams on 28 lines.

Carbon Thongs ™ is a logo used to depict a window of information on consumer goods and services which give consumers an idea of the carbon footprint of that product or service, they use. The carbon footprint thong is coloured in green and black with a percentage % measure to indicate the amount of environmental impact, that product or service has, on the environment.

"To promote and support excellence in travelling with public transport in Victoria."

Keolis Downers's guiding principle is to 'think like a passenger'. Inspired to make your journey the best possible travelling experience. Delivering a holistic approach to using Public Transport Victoria (PTV). Ensuring all passengers can make informed choices, have access to reliable services, enjoy a safe 'Zero Harm' and clean travelling environment and be provided with elevated levels of customer service.

Certificate

of **myki** Excellence

86 To Bundoora RMIT

27 Westgarth St
26 Walker St
25 Clifton Hill Interchange
23 Wellington St
22 Grant St*
21 Alexandra Pde*
20 Keele St
19 Johnston St
13 Brunswick St
12 Melbourne Museum*
11 Victoria Pde*
10 Parliament Station
4 Bourke St Mall
1 Southern Cross Station

86 To Waterfront City Docklands

Routes and symbols

86	Tram route number		Accessible tram stop
---	Tram lines		No trams
	Train connection		Tram replacement bus
	Night Network		

Not to scale, not all stops shown
* Replacement buses will not service these stops

A holistic approach, contributing to the economic and environmental sustainability of our city, as well as help strengthen our local communities.

We want all passengers to feel confident when using the network, especially on different routes or in unfamiliar areas. Passengers will know where to buy a ticket, be able to identify the nearest stop and know when the next tram service is due.

We will work with the government, Public Transport Victoria and other transport operators to provide a fully integrated transport offer to the people of Melbourne

REUSE

again

and again

on all

Trams,

Trains

and Buses

in Melbourne

and Country

Victoria

Keep your **MYKI**

Safe in this pocket

Hi, I'm Lenny the Tram Driver,
Terry the Tram and I, are
going to take you on
a marvellous journey, along
Route 86, let's get ready........

Before you go to the tram stop,

lets do a quick check,

✔ Bag

✔ Hat

✔ MYKI card

Terry and I'll be along soon.

Keep an eye out and you'll see us

coming, along the track.

Look, Terry Tram is not far away.
He is as big as an asphalt tip
truck, bigger than a car and
as strong and heavy, as a big,
horned rhinoceros.

But, stay back till he gets here.
Don't walk out yet.

Soon, Terry will be right here.
Let's look out for cars, bicycles
and motorbikes, to make sure they
have completely, stopped.
The lights are flashing orange.
Time to approach Terry the Tram.
Lenny the driver has opened his
doors. Board quickly.

Tap your MYKI on the handi – hand.

Bing- Successful Touch On.

Choose a nice window seat

and sit on a comfy green chair.

There may be many people on the tram. Some will be reading, others listening to music or catching up, with friends. Gazing out the window, at all the sights, is so exciting. There is so much fun to be had, riding on Terry Tram.

Hey, there's Lenny the tram driver. He sits in his own seat and looks very happy. His cabin has many buttons and knobs but where is his steering wheel? How does Terry go around corners?

Oh! he rides on his tracks. The tracks are made of steel and always stuck in the ground. Terry can only travel where there are tracks and overhead electrical power.

If a car in on the tracks, Terry has to stop and wait. He cannot go around and he cannot push past. We all have to wait for the tracks to clear, before we can move forward again. And on we go again... go Terry go...

Route 86 will turn right off Smith St and into Gertrude Street. At Stop 14, you'll see the Fitzroy 20 storey flats. They are tall and look like a Lego building. They were built in the 1960s.

First, they dug a deep hole, as deep as they are high. Then a big crane lifted each panel up, one by one, piece by piece and placed them into position.

Keep an eye out for your hop off Tram stop. It is written on the Tram stop sign, way up high! All the tram stops are the same colours and have their own number, to let you know where you are. Here's Stop 13 on the corner of Gertrude Street and Brunswick Street, Fitzroy.

Before you get off! "STOP Terry this is my stop!" OK, time to be MINDFUL now people. Don't panic. Look around you and find the small green STOP button and press it. "Bing" goes the Bell and Lenny's head lights up. Hold on tight... you're about to feel Terry Tram's Superpower brakes...screech and smoke! Phew! "Well done", haha! laughs Lenny. You just brought the whole of Terry Tram to a complete stop with your Super Finger."

Before you leave the tram, check that you have all your belongings. Don't forget to Touch Off with your MYKI card. Make your way to the exit door and wait, for the Tram to stop.

Find the small green STOP button on any nearby pole.

Lenny the Tram driver, will stop at the Tram stop and the Red traffic lights. The doors will open, check all is clear and you can leave the tram safely!

Everybody waits for the traffic lights. Terry waits, cars wait, bicycles wait. When the lights go Green, farewell Terry with a hearty,

"Go!! Terry"

Fitzroy has many historical sights and I enjoy the walk to the corner of Brunswick St and Victoria Parade. I walk past the Greek Agean Tavern, The Catholic University and some lovely terraces. One has a big magnolia tree out front.

It is very busy here. I can see

St Patrick's Catherdaral long spire

streching up to the clouds.

The Eye and Ear hospital, St Vincent's

hospital and the Old Melbourne

Firestation Museum are here too.

All on one corner.

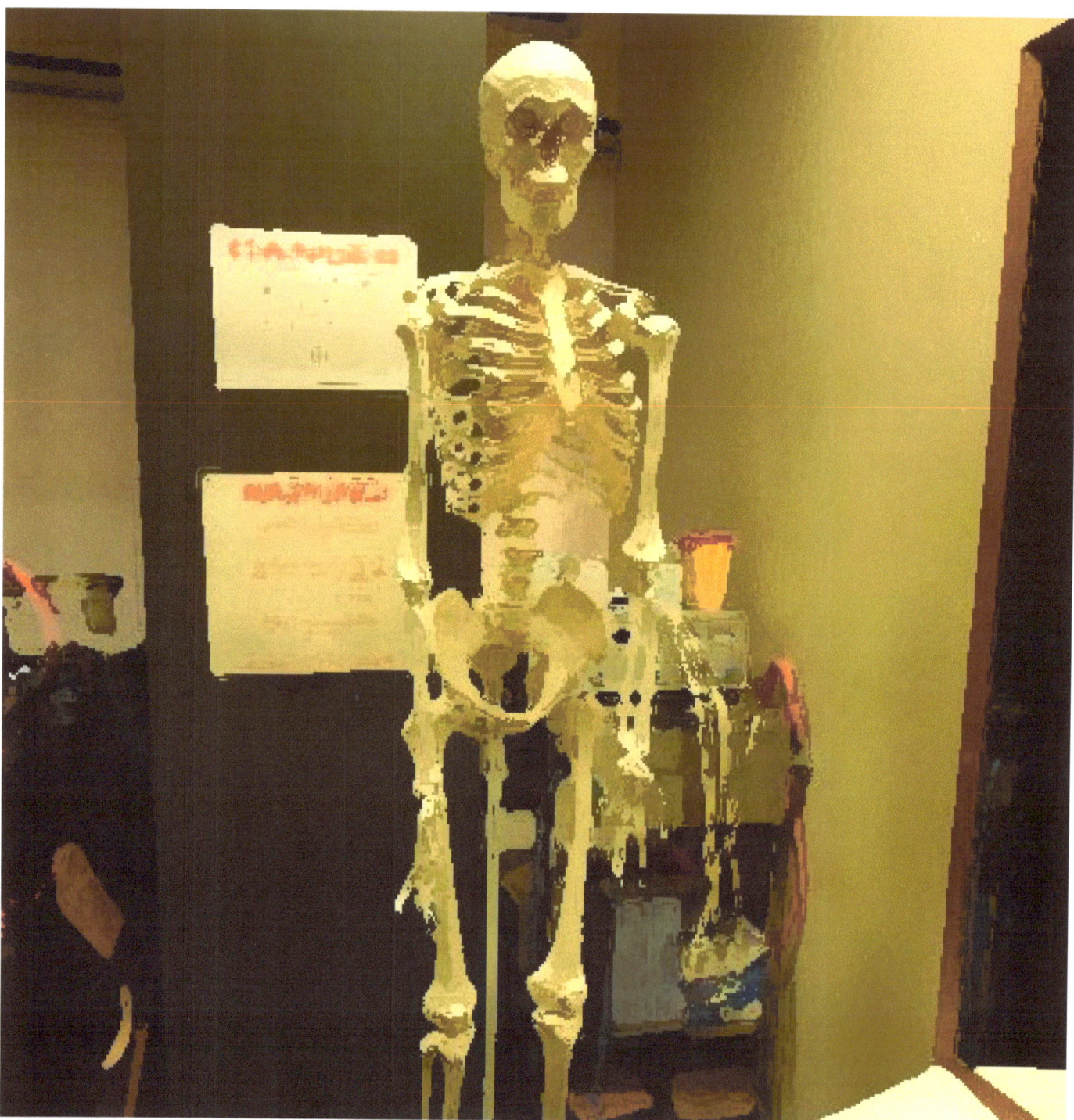

I arrive on time for my appointment with Dr Jawbone. The receptionist is waiting for me.

"How do you do?", I ask when she calls me in to her doctor's surgery. There are always many interesting things to see there.

The Response car, with its white, green and orange panels, is always near by, should Terry need help, too!

The End

Fun Stuff To Do: Miss Cactus Opunti's Travel Activities

G'day Travellers, your Tram Teacher, Miss Opunti has some fun learning tasks for you to complete along your journey. Have a go yourself, then, flip to the back of the book and check your answers. You Can Do It !

FORCES QUESTIONS: **FORCES** that work on objects including Terry Tram are **Push** and **Pull**:

A Acts on the ball

B Acts on the fish

C Acts on the cart

D Acts on the dog

E Acts on the wheelborrow

F Acts on the sock

Check your Answers:

Forces ANSWERS:

- Starting and object moving =E
- Stopping and object moving = D
- Changing the direction of movement= A
- Balancing another force,
  and preventing movement = F
- Bending an object = B

Liveability Crossword

Across

(6) How much you spend is known as your _____.

(7) The quality of the natural environment depends on 5 key elements, including _____.

(8) The _____ environment refers to any human-made structure, facility or service.

(9) Access to _____ housing is an indicator of the liveability of the built environment.

(10) A term that describes a community's quality of life is _____.

(11) How much it costs to pay for necessities like food, rent, bills and transport is known as the _____ of living.

(12) Financial stability refers to _____ wellbeing.

Down

(1) An example of the natural environment is a _____.

(2) Social _____ refers to how safe and happy people feel within their community.

(3) The most liveable places in the world provide quality _____ to all citizens.

(4) _____ wages are controlled by governments to protect workers and ensure they are paid enough to cover the cost of living.

(5) The liveability of a place is affected by how accessible places of cultural, entertainment and _____ importance are to the people who live there.

(9) A liveable community is one where people feel connected and safe, and where the _____ is spread evenly throughout the community.

(12) The liveability of a place can be broken down into 3 key areas: social wellbeing, economic wellbeing and _____ wellbeing.

Liveability Crossword **Answers**

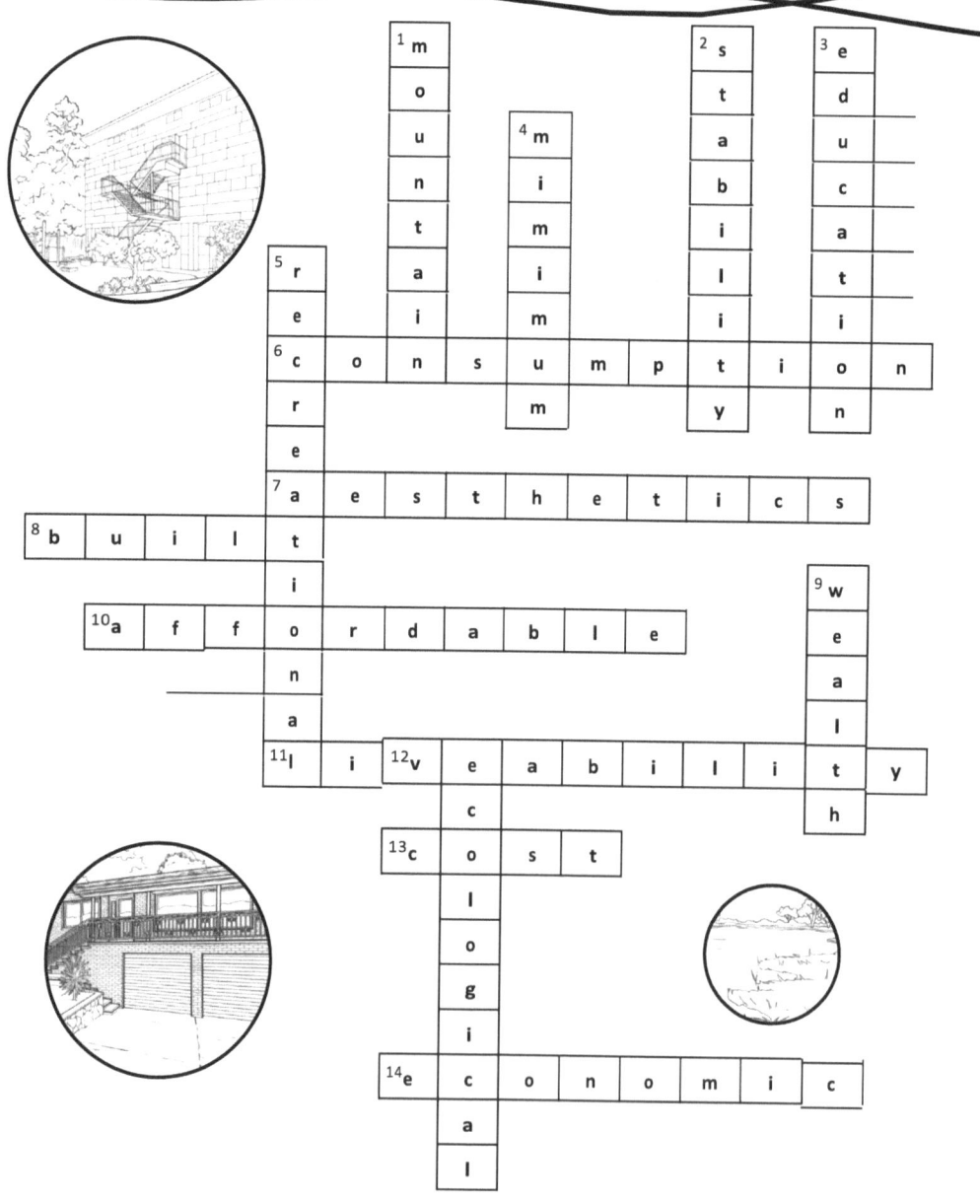

1 Down: mountain

4 Down: mimimm

2 Down: stability

3 Down: education

5 Down: recreation

6 Across: consumption

7 Across: aesthetics

8 Across: built

10 Across: affordable

9 Down: wealth

11 Across / 12 Down: liveability

12 Down: vcological

13 Across: cost

14 Across: economic

Across

(6) How much you spend is known as your **consumption**.

(7) The quality of the natural environment depends on 5 key elements, including **aesthetics**.

(8) The **built** environment refers to any human-made structure, facility or service.

(9) Access to **affordable** housing is an indicator of the liveability of the built environment.

(10) A term that describes a community's quality of life is **liveability**.

(11) How much it costs to pay for necessities like food, rent, bills and transport is known as the **cost** of living.

(12) Financial stability refers to **economic** wellbeing.

Down

(1) An example of the natural environment is a **mountain**.

(2) Social **stability** refers to how safe and happy people feel within their community.

(3) The most liveable places in the world provide quality **education** to all citizens.

(4) **Minimum** wages are controlled by governments to protect workers and ensure they are paid enough to cover the cost of living.

(5) The liveability of a place is affected by how accessible places of cultural, entertainment and **recreational** importance are to the people who live there.

(9) A liveable community is one where people feel connected and safe, and where the **wealth** is spread evenly throughout the community.

(12) The liveability of a place can be broken down into 3 key areas: social wellbeing, economic wellbeing and **ecological** wellbeing.

About the Author:

R. Lazar from Downunder. A bilingual Australian – Greek teacher, with a Master of Education from Melbourne University. Passionate RRR subscriber and Biological Scientist working together towards building and preserving sustainable habitats for future generations of Fauna and Flora. Strong believer in a God who dislikes waste; and is 'The Great Recycler of All'. From baby seeds in a patch of dirt, to huge oak trees, to generous leaves that compost and provide tender green grasslands.

www.ingramcontent.com/pod-product-compliance
Lightning Source LLC
Chambersburg PA
CBHW041433120626
46547CB00002B/193